GROUNDBREAKER BIOS

Frida Kahlo

BY KATE CONLEY

CONTENT CONSULTANT
LEONARD FOLGARAIT, PhD
DISTINGUISHED PROFESSOR OF HISTORY OF ART
VANDERBILT UNIVERSITY

Kids Core
An Imprint of Abdo Publishing
abdobooks.com

abdobooks.com

Published by Abdo Publishing, a division of ABDO, PO Box 398166, Minneapolis, Minnesota 55439.

Printed in the United States of America, North Mankato, Minnesota.
102021
012022

THIS BOOK CONTAINS RECYCLED MATERIALS

Cover Photo: Bettmann/Getty Images
Interior Photos: Vintage_Space/Alamy, 4–5; Gisele Freund/Photo Researchers History/Getty Images, 6, 28 (right); Dom Slike/Alamy, 8; GL Archive/Alamy, 10, 26, 28 (left); Agencia el Universal/GDA/AP Images, 12–13; Anton Ivanov/Shutterstock Images, 14; Bettmann/Getty Images, 16, 29 (bottom); Red Line Editorial, 18; John MacDougall/AFP/Getty Images, 20–21, 29 (top); Thomas Peters/Reuters/Alamy, 22; Guy Bell/Alamy, 24

Editor: Ann Schwab
Series Designer: Christine Ha

Library of Congress Control Number: 2021941509

Publisher's Cataloging-in-Publication Data

Names: Conley, Kate, author.
Title: Frida Kahlo / by Kate Conley
Description: Minneapolis, Minnesota : Abdo Publishing, 2022 | Series: Groundbreaker bios | Includes online resources and index.
Identifiers: ISBN 9781532196850 (lib. bdg.) | ISBN 9781644946695 (pbk.) | ISBN 9781098218669 (ebook)
Subjects: LCSH: Kahlo, Frida--Juvenile literature. | Women painters--Biography--Juvenile literature. | Women artists--Biography--Juvenile literature. | Painting, Mexican--Juvenile literature. | Women political activists--Biography--Juvenile literature.
Classification: DDC 759.972 [B]--dc23

CONTENTS

Frida Kahlo is considered one of Mexico's greatest artists.

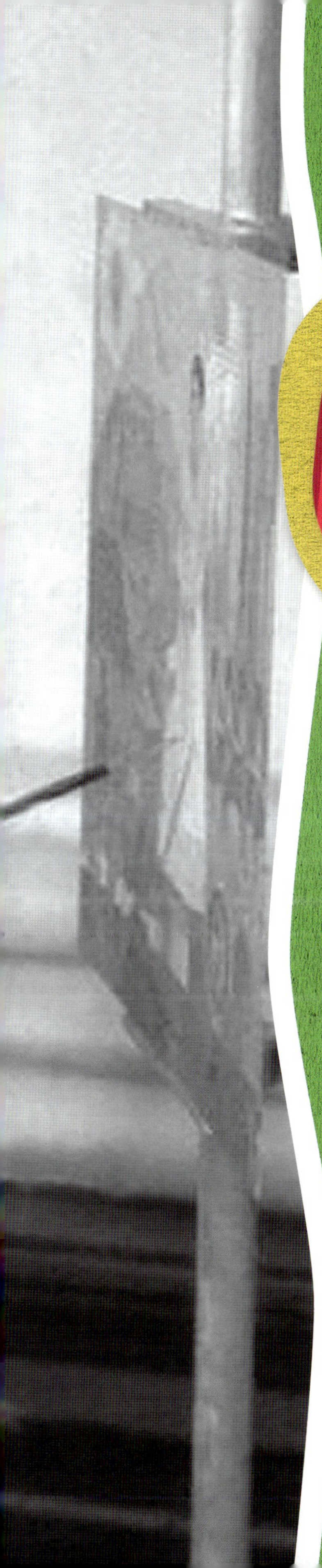

CHAPTER 1

Who Was Frida Kahlo?

In April 1953, Lola Álvarez Bravo held an art show in Mexico City, Mexico. It displayed works by Frida Kahlo, Bravo's friend. Kahlo was a famous artist in other parts of the world. But this was her first **solo** art show in her own country.

Frida Kahlo had many health issues during her life. Because of this, she often spent time in bed.

Kahlo wanted to attend, but she was unwell. Her doctors had ordered her to stay in bed. But Kahlo refused to miss the opening night. She hired an ambulance to take her there. Her four-poster bed from home was set up at the show.

More than 200 guests attended the opening night. From her bed, Kahlo visited with guests. She ate, drank, and sang with them. It was a high point in Kahlo's career. But it had not come easily. Kahlo faced many challenges, especially with her health. Despite this, she never stopped painting.

Frida's childhood was filled with difficulties such as illness and political unrest.

Frida's Childhood

Frida was born on July 6, 1907, in the Coyoacán area of Mexico City. Her father, Guillermo, was a photographer. Her mother, Matilde, ran the home.

Frida had two older sisters and one younger sister. The Kahlos lived in a home called *La Casa Azul*. It means “The Blue House” in Spanish.

When Frida was three, the Mexican Revolution started. It impacted most of Frida’s childhood. She could hear bullets screech past the windows of her home. Sometimes soldiers arrived at La Casa Azul. Frida’s mother would feed them and care for the wounded.

A New Birthday

Frida often told people she was born in 1910 even though it was not true. That was the year the Mexican Revolution started. She liked to think of herself and modern Mexico as beginning in the same year.

Frida, *right*, grew up with with her sisters, Cristina, Matilde, and Adriana.

When Frida was six, she got an illness called polio. She had to stay in bed for nine months. Polio weakened her right leg and foot. It left her with a limp. Her father helped her to rebuild the strength in her leg. He encouraged her to be active. She liked to swim, ride bicycles, skate, and wrestle.

Primary Source

Frida Kahlo suffered from pain in her body most of her life. She used painting to help her through it. At the end of her life, she said:

> I am not sick. I am broken. But I am happy to be alive as long as I can paint.

Source: *The Life and Times of Frida Kahlo*. Directed by Amy Stechler, Daylight Films and WETA Washington, 2005.

What's the Big Idea?

Read this quote carefully. What is its main idea? Explain how the main idea is supported by details.

Diego Rivera was a famous painter known for his colorful murals.

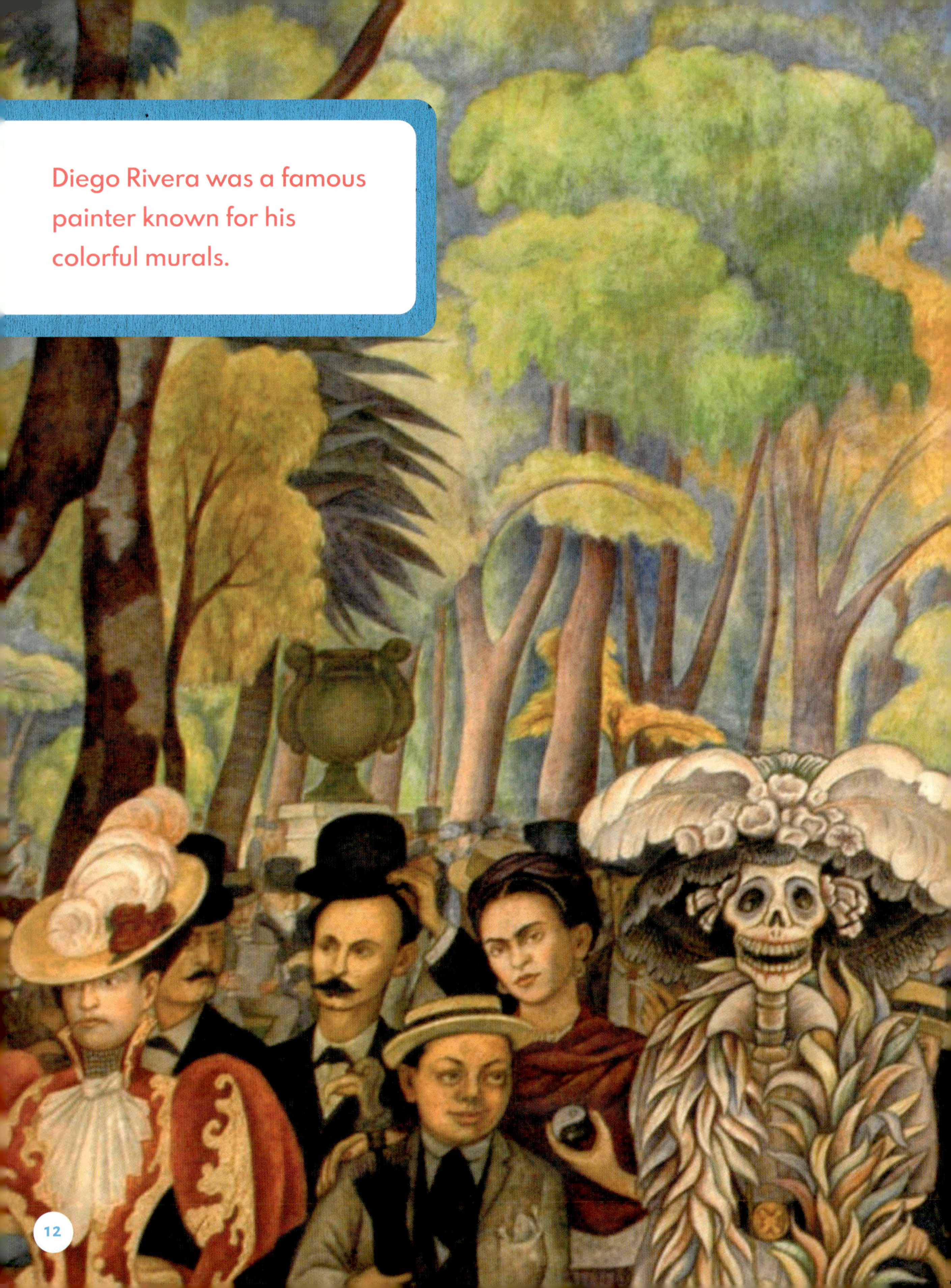

CHAPTER 2

Learning to Paint

When Frida was 15, she began classes at the National Preparatory School. It was the best high school in Mexico. She was one of its first female students. While there, Frida met an artist named Diego Rivera.

Some of Frida's paints and brushes are on display at La Casa Azul, which is now a museum dedicated to her.

He was painting a **mural** inside the school. Frida and her friends liked to watch him work.

Frida studied hard and hoped to be a doctor one day. But her plans changed suddenly on

September 17, 1925. That day, Frida was riding on a bus that got into an accident. She broke many bones, including several in her spine. Doctors were not sure if she would live.

Frida spent months recovering at La Casa Azul. She had to spend long periods of time in bed as her body healed. She also had to wear a cast on her **torso** to support her spine. To pass the time, she taught herself to paint.

Self-Portraits

Kahlo made 143 paintings in her career. Fifty-five of them were self-portraits. They are some of her best-known works.

Frida Kahlo and her husband, Diego Rivera, experienced many challenges in their marriage.

A New Phase

By 1927, Kahlo's injuries had improved. But she struggled with health issues for the rest of her life. She became involved in politics and also reconnected with Rivera. She showed him some of her art. Rivera thought she was talented. He urged her to keep painting. The two quickly became friends and then married in 1929.

The couple moved to the United States in November 1930. They lived there for the next three years. Rivera painted several murals in that time. But Kahlo faced many challenges. She lost her unborn baby, and then her mother died. She was lonely and homesick. Kahlo expressed her pain through her art.

Frida Kahlo and Diego Rivera spent much of the early 1930s in the United States. They traveled from city to city wherever Rivera had work painting murals. They lived in San Francisco, California; Detroit, Michigan; and New York City, New York.

Rivera and Kahlo returned to Mexico in late 1933. It was an unhappy time for them. Injuries from the bus accident still caused her pain. Rivera and Kahlo separated for a short time in 1935. Through all the troubles, Kahlo kept painting.

Explore Online

Visit the website below. Does it give any new information about Kahlo's artwork that wasn't in Chapter Two?

Frida Kahlo

abdocorelibrary.com/frida-kahlo

Kahlo's painting "Self-Portrait as a Tehuana or Diego on My Mind" was included in an exhibit at a museum in Berlin, Germany.

CHAPTER 3

An Artistic Success

In 1937, Kahlo displayed her work in public for the first time. She submitted four paintings to a group art show. They received praise. One of the people who attended the show was Julien Levy.

Many of Kahlo's self-portraits included a black cat, a symbol of bad luck.

Levy owned an art **gallery** in New York City. Kahlo's work caught his attention. Levy worked with **surrealist** art. This combines images of fantasy with reality. Levy thought Kahlo's paintings had many surrealist images. He displayed her paintings in his gallery in 1938. It was her first solo art show, and it was a great success.

Kahlo then received an offer from André Breton. He was a French poet and one of the founders of surrealism. He asked Kahlo to exhibit her work in Paris, France. She agreed. Painter Marcel Duchamp organized the art show. Once again, Kahlo's work received high praise.

Some of Kahlo's paintings were included in an exhibition called "From Selfie to Self-Expression" at the Saatchi Gallery in London, United Kingdom.

Fame

Kahlo then returned to Mexico. She had changed. Kahlo was no longer just the wife of a famous artist. She was a respected artist herself.

She had developed her own style, especially with her self-portraits. She usually painted herself with a single dark eyebrow or unibrow, a faint mustache, and flowers in her hair.

Kahlo was very successful. But her life was still hard. She and Rivera divorced in November 1939. She underwent many surgeries to help with her pain. Her health was poor.

Communism

Aside from painting, Kahlo and Rivera shared a passion for politics. They both supported **communism**. Their home became a safe place for communist leaders who faced troubles in their home countries.

Frida Kahlo has become one of the world's most beloved artists.

Rivera and Kahlo remarried in 1940. Two years later, Kahlo began to teach painting. She soon became too ill to travel to the school. The students came to her house for lessons. She also continued her own paintings. But her body was growing weaker. She died on July 13, 1954. In the time since then, she has become one of the world's best-known and loved painters.

Further Evidence

Look at the website below. Does it give any new evidence to support Chapter Three?

The Life and Times of Frida Kahlo

abdocorelibrary.com/frida-kahlo

Timeline

1907
Frida Kahlo is born in Mexico on July 6.

1913
Kahlo gets polio. The disease damages her leg and foot and leaves her with a limp.

1922
Kahlo begins classes at the National Preparatory School in Mexico City.

1925
A bus accident leaves Kahlo badly injured, and she teaches herself to paint as she recovers.

1938
Kahlo has her first solo art exhibition.

1929
Kahlo marries Diego Rivera, a famous Mexican mural painter.

1954
After suffering poor health for most of her life, Kahlo dies on July 13.

Glossary

communism
a system in which the government owns all of a nation's land, property, and businesses so the citizens can share the resources equally

gallery
a room or building that is used to display or sell art

mural
a large painting that is created directly on a wall

solo
something done by a single person

surrealist
describing a style of art that combines images of fantasy with reality

torso
the trunk of a person's body, which includes the chest, back, and stomach

Online Resources

To learn more about Frida Kahlo, visit our free resource websites below.

Core Library CONNECTION
FREE! COMMON CORE MULTIMEDIA RESOURCES

Visit **abdocorelibrary.com** or scan this QR code for free Common Core resources for teachers and students, including vetted activities, multimedia, and booklinks, for deeper subject comprehension.

Booklinks NONFICTION NETWORK
FREE! ONLINE NONFICTION RESOURCES

Visit **abdobooklinks.com** or scan this QR code for free additional online weblinks for further learning. These links are routinely monitored and updated to provide the most current information available.

Learn More

Buckley, James, Jr. *Frida Kahlo: The Revolutionary Painter!* Portable, 2021.

Kahlo, Frida. *The Two Fridas.* Schiffer, 2021.

Index

About the Author

Kate Conley has been writing nonfiction books for children for more than ten years. When she's not writing, Conley spends her time reading, sewing, and solving crossword puzzles. She lives in Minnesota with her husband and two children.